DATE DUE			
JE 02 '94			

Creepy Crawly Critter Riddles

Joanne E. Bernstein & Paul Cohen
pictures by Rosekrans Hoffman

Albert Whitman & Company, Niles, Illinois

Also by Joanne E. Bernstein & Paul Cohen
Happy Holiday Riddles to You
More Unidentified Flying Riddles
Un-Frog-Gettable Riddles
Unidentified Flying Riddles
What Was the Wicked Witch's Real Name?
and Other Character Riddles

Library of Congress Cataloging-in-Publication Data

Bernstein, Joanne E.
Creepy crawly critter riddles.

Summary: An illustrated collection of more than
eighty jokes and riddles about ants, bees, spiders,
octopi, and other animals that crawl or slither.
1. Riddles, Juvenile. 2. Animals—Juvenile humor.
[1. Animals—Wit and humor. 2. Riddles. 3. Jokes]
I. Cohen, Paul, 1945- . II. Hoffman, Rosekrans,
ill. III. Title.
PN6371.5.B394 1986 818'.5402   86-15911
ISBN 0-8075-1345-8

Text © 1986 by Joanne E. Bernstein and Paul Cohen
Illustrations © 1986 by Rosekrans Hoffman
Published in 1986 by Albert Whitman & Company, Niles, Illinois
Published simultaneously in Canada
by General Publishing, Limited, Toronto
10   9   8   7   6   5   4   3   2

THE CRITTERS' CRAWL OF FAME

Who was the greatest insect baseball player?
Mickey Mantis.

Who are the best-dressed insects on the police force?
The Miami Lice.

Who is the crabs' favorite comedian?
Bill Clawsby.

Who is the termites' favorite comedian?
Woody Allen.

Which mosquito attacked Dorothy and Toto?
The Wicked Itch of the West.

What do you call a snake who's a perfect "Ten"?
Boa Derek.

Who can leap tall poodles in a single bound?
Super Flea.

OFF-THE-WALL RIDDLES

Where do spiders go to learn new words?
Web-ster's Dictionary.

What's the difference between a duck and a spider?
The duck has a web in its feet; the spider has its feet in a web.

Why are spiders good baseball players?
Because they know how to catch flies.

How does a spider greet a fly?
"I'm so pleased to eat you!"

First mother fly: How's the new baby?
**Second mother fly: Very restless. I had to walk
the ceiling with him all night.**

**What's more dangerous than the eensy-weensy
spider?**
The teensy tsetse fly.

How do you swat flies in Texas?
With a tennis racket.

What happened to the spider's TV show?
It produced spin-offs.

Where do flies go in the wintertime?
I don't know, but I wish they'd go there in the
summertime, too.

Why do we need window screens?
So flies can't escape.

Customer: Waiter, what is that fly doing in my
   alphabet soup?
Waiter: Learning to read, sir.

Customer: Waiter, there's a fly in my chop suey.
Waiter: That's nothing. Wait until you see what's
   in your fortune cookie.

Customer: Waiter, there's a fly in my soup!
Waiter: Shh—everyone will want one!

TINY TERRORS

Do ants have brains?
Of course. How else would they figure out when
   you're having a picnic?

**What is the most popular word game in the ant
   colony?**
Buggle.

Which insect handles your questions, Madam?
An ant, Sir.

Why should you never invite termites to dine?
Because they'll eat you out of house and home.

What do termites eat for dessert?
Toothpicks.

What are French ticks called?
Paris-ites.

**What do you get when you cross a praying
mantis with a termite?**
A bug that says grace before eating your house.

Why did Mama Flea look so sad?
All her children were going to the dogs.

What do fleas do in the winter?
Fleeze!

If you find two bugs in a cotton boll, which should you choose?
Always choose the lesser of two weevils.

Knock, knock.
Who's there?
Weevil.
Weevil who?
Weevil see you later.

CRAWL SPACE

Did you hear about the little worm who joined the army?
No, what about him?
He's in the Apple Corps (core).

Why can't you find nightcrawlers in the winter?
They only come out in worm weather.

Why did the worm decide to sleep late?
Because he didn't want the early bird to catch him.

What's spiral in shape and very crowded?
A snail with a house guest.

What is the slowest way to send a letter?
The U.S. Snail.

Why was the inchworm angry?
He had to convert to the metric system.

What did the robin say when his food went bad?
"The worm has turned."

Why was the slug arrested?
Because he tried to get into the parking meter.

HUM-DINGERS

How do we know bees watch TV?
They have antennae.

What did the male bee call his darling queen?
Honey.

Which bee can't buzz?
The mumblebee.

What melody do bees like in stormy weather?
"Stingin' in the Rain."

What do bees hum on their way back to the hive?
"Bee it ever so bumble, there's no place like comb."

What did one bee say to her nosy neighbor?
"Mind your own bee's wax."

What do you call a confused bumblebee?
Buzzled.

Which is the favorite soap opera back at the nest?
General Waspital.

What do you get when you cross a bumblebee with a bell?
A humdinger.

What do bees do with their honey?
They cell it.

What causes hives?
Bees.

Which is the most musical hive?
The bee flat.

Which bees are always complaining about their food?
The honeymoaners.

PEST EXPERIENCES

When do roaches use the telephone?
When they want to crawl long distance.

What insect crows at sunrise?
A cockroach.

What do cooties use to clean their houses?
Lice-all.

Why did the cootie have to go to traffic court?
He was driving without a lice-ense.

What do you call frozen cooties?
Licicles.

What is the richest insect family?
The Roachefellers.

What does a louse call his girl friend?
Cootie pie.

Why do louse families get along so well?
They're close-nit.

ALL-A-FLUTTER

Have you ever seen a butterfly cry?
No, but I've seen a moth bawl.

Why do moth actors fly toward candles?
They want to be flame-ous.

Why do moths read adventure stories?
They enjoy a good yarn.

How do you milk a caterpillar?
First you find a very low stool.

Definition of a butterfly: A worm that's won its wings.

What has a hundred legs but can't walk?
Fifty pairs of pants. Fooled you!

What do you call a fly that's lost its job?
A fired-fly.

Why do fireflies do especially well in school?
Because they're so bright.

FANGS FOR THE MEMORIES

How can you tell a baby snake?
By its rattle.

Which snake wears a hard hat?
A boa constructor.

How do you turn a wasp into a snake?
Take away its "w." Then it's an asp.

Where do snakes ski?
Asp-en.

Which snake do you find on your vindshield?
A vindow viper.

What do snakes give their moms on Mother's Day?
Hugs and hisses.

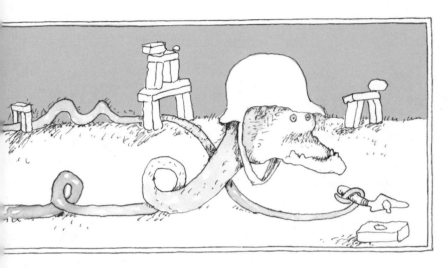

What do you get when you cross a snake with a kangaroo?
A jump rope.

What do you get when you cross a rattlesnake with a doughnut?
A snake, rattle, and roll.

Why do we forgive large snakes?
We let pythons be pythons.

Why can't you hear a cobra coming?
It just snakes up on you.

Sidney Snake: I'm glad I'm not poisonous.
Sherry Snake: Why?
Sidney: Because I just bit my tongue.

SEA-LEBRITIES

How does a lobster get from place to place?
By taxi-crab.

What do you call someone who eats all the clams?
Shellfish!

What holiday honors shellfish?
Oyster Sunday.

What word game do shellfish like best?
Crabble.

Where can you get cash for your shrimps?
In a prawn shop.

Why does the ocean roar?
You would, too, if you had lobsters in your bed.

Where do jellyfish get their jelly?
From ocean currents (currants).

**What do you get when you cross an octopus
with a typewriter?**
No one knows, but it types eight hundred words a
minute.

**What do you get when you cross a chicken and
an octopus?**
Drumsticks for everyone.

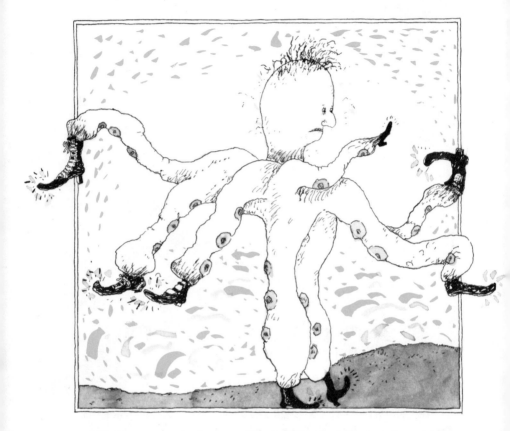

What goes ouch, ouch, ouch, ouch, ouch, ouch, ouch, ouch?
An octopus wearing tight shoes.

What does an octopus wear on a cold day?
A coat of arms.

Do octopi like Trix?
No, silly. Trix are for squids.

FEATURED CREATURES

What happened to Sir Galahad the Worm when he fell off his horse?
He became a knightcrawler.

What famous insect flies into the fireplace?
Chim-i-ney Cricket.

Where do you read about Hercules the Caterpillar?
In Greek Mothology.

Why was Miss Muffet's spider such a nuisance?
It kept getting in the whey.

Who hopped around the wild frontier?
Davey Cricket.

Which Confederate general rode a dog?
Robert E. Flea.

Who was Robert E. Flea's opponent?
Ulysses S. Ant.

Who ferries roaches across the stream?
Bugboat Annie.

Which creepy crawler does Nancy like?
Slug-go.

Which snake had tea with Alice in Wonderland?
The Mad Adder.

Which famous melody is about a clumsy insect?
"Flight of the Fumblebee."

BUGGIN' AROUND

How do Hollywood bugs get into the house?
They pass a screen test.

**What does the producer tell the bugs after the
  screen test?**
"Don't crawl us, we'll crawl you."

Which fantasy game do insects enjoy?
Dungeons and dragonflies.

Who are the perfect mates for a man-tis?
A ladybug or a damselfly.

What comes after a mayfly?
A June bug.

Why did the spy call an exterminator?
Because he thought the room was bugged.

What insect goes "Hee-haw, hee-haw"?
A braying mantis.

What do you get when you cross two insects and a rabbit?
Bugs Bunny.

How do insects get the news?
From the flypaper.

What's the best way to avoid biting insects?
Keep your mouth closed.